POETRY FROM MY HEART

SANJANA

ISBN 979-888546439-0

Contents

Preface

I am author of this book , feel very glad that now finally the time has arrived which I was looking for a long time, by publishing my book. I am not a professional writer, trying to exaggerate my feelings through my poems. I have written this book from my heart, it incorporate many poems in different genres, some poems tells lots of deep thoughts which actually worthwhile. you will find some of the poetry says stories and momentos that I hope will touch your heart.

1. The Rainy Night

You're coming to me quietly!
Still, I can't guess why are you staying silent this much?
I sometime astonished with this thought
That you sometimes become halcyon and sometimes explosive
as yell,
The aesthetically pleasing scene which you create aftermath
invade my breathing.
The echo which you drops form somehow embrace you to me.
I want this momentum going on until I perish eternally
I just wanna feel you on my face
Let's dance with me, don't need to scare from this,
Just feel the rhythm of the aura of surrounding
Let give space to others and come with me.
I want to know about you more than yours
I want from you to wash my sorrow,
And let away my pain and leave me with endure delightment
Its you falling but yet no one can feel you
Except me, only I can hear you
Let's make today together until everyone awake
Let's cherish this night till my last breath.

2. Nighty Night

Day comes which I want
Something I flaunt
But what can I do
Nothing is my fault
My dream comes short
I scream and awake
No one shown except one who me shake
I turned towards
Then go forwards
I have chased
A confused smile comes on my face
I don't know who is she?
Only know she look likes me I asked her who are you?
She didn't say a word
Soon it gets blurred
Something strikes in my mind
Suddenly I come to realise she was nobody but my look-alike.
Aside was a letter
It consist you do much more better
Broad smile comes on
I didn't know why I was smiling more?
Something I get
which I really want

It's one which everyone needs
But no one concede
Now I intellect that
If I do anything confidently
I'll definitely get good result consequently.
I feels more in my eyes now a blooming light
I come to know it's for me nighty night.

3. Shackled Fear

I won't be afraid of myself
though, I am afraid from darkness.
Want to break all the shackles.
I don't know how I can fly,
Fear surrounde me
Whenever I keep it away from myself.
It comes back again.
I've lost myself somewhere.
I failed to find myself no matter how hard I try.
fear has taken away my words.
I usually keep myself calm.
But for how long?
I'm tired now
Fear that doesn't let live.
I know this word has a deep meaning
But the deeper it means,
the more it leaves its mark.
fear can be cruel,
It leaves the soul
but never leaves the heart in the soul.
It same happens with me.
I can't resist it.
The more we run away from it.

the more it runs to us.

Hey! it's enough to say

Now I wanna go to that world where I scared to fear.

4. A Moon on Ridge

Was tranquility!
Only seems a moon having Ray's of white shades,
It's alluring but little bit faded,
Nature overwraped the wonder of beauty,
Nothing left having sky seems sooty,
Tremendous scene, horrific look
Everyone shook!
Hereafter, things calm down,
Surrounding atmosphere seems something glower.
One thing still silent,
Glossy or fixed.
"None other than the moon stay
Straight upward on the ridge."

5. Corruption A Curse

Corruption is now become a profession,
It always set in minds of all
But no one Acknowledge it's true sense.
Some of them concede it or some don't be.
It spread across in the well maintained thoughts of people just
like as infection,
That's the reason why it need proper medication.
We hardly raise a voice against it.
We wanna erode it but couldn't.
Why it happens?
Bcoz In sudden urge of thrills,
we quills our mind according to our wills
Root cause are "we".
We don't let it out
Inspite of it we let in.
It's a type of termite
Never leaves people day or night.
We shouldn't relinquishing
Until and unless we drive it away By skirmishing.
Let's pledge together to make it out from our life.
Otherwise it smashed everything like knife.

6. The Reality of life

If you think you are beaten, you are,

If you think you dare not, you don't.

If you'd like to win but you think you can't,

It's almost a lost!

If you think you'll lose, you've lost,

for out in this world we find success begins,

with your wish and this all of in the state of mind.

life is a battle,

you change your personality and the person that has a state of mind WHO ARE SUCCESS...

7. Can Someone Be?

Can anyone be so selfless?

Their work so commandable

Do anyone see inside their heart?

How much they feel helpless?

Can anyone discern?

They too are humans.

Who sacrifices themselves

Only for ourselves.

Everyone can see the pride bloom in their eyes

But can anyone be the first one who see in their eyes the
battle with which they fight all the time?

Can anyone see that they renounced their Festivals to serve
the country?

But no one even examine their sombre life going through the
whole journey.

Should I fight or shouldn't?

They never waste their minutes.

They fight for their nations welfare.

But are we always with them fair?

We break the rules yet do we think

No we don't atleast at one.

We also know that they work more hard on borders

But can we think how harsh it would be to work continuously

without even taking break or breaking the orders?

If none is able to ensure themselves

Take out time and put your mind and think will it not be right that we should give respect to such selfless people which they deserve.

And don't even think about their life that this has to be preserve.

8. Guess what's this actually?

The pureness with which it lives,
My eyes can't see
Is it aligned with innocence
which can't clarified.
I think
God divided it out
Just for me
I wish I could see it from day to night.
But is it possible?
It's a wonder of beauty
My eyes to behold
Happiness for the youngsters
And promise for the old
A creation from spectrum
Reflection of light
Made from backdrops
Cheerful and bright.
Arch in the sky
Gift of the god
It formed so rare
"What it is?
Can anyone share."

9. Mirror and you!!

If you see in the mirror
What you would see,
The face which Enunciate your life clearly.
Your displeasure, hypocrisy, anger and what not.
But would it reads your mind
Would it exaggerate,
How You had struggled
It shows you a benevolent person
Your everything about your nature
Nevertheless, would it say how did you become like this.
I guess probably not.
Accurately you're your own mirror
You are the true mirror of yours
You can observe your deeds
And change it as appropriately.
"Mirror shows you what it sees but what you know mirror can't see."

10. Desert Heat!

The desert heat I can't cease
It's something I never see.
Up from the ground into my feet,
But alas, I can't cease
I wish I could succeed.
This is like a hunter
I wish I would face it if I was like it.
This eats my body like a Ravenous creature.
I wish It didn't reach me
It cut me like a sharp knife.
It mercilessly takes my life.

11. BEAUTY AND THE BEAST!

A beast dwell in an enchanted castle

A most hideous person live here

No place for hustle and bustle

Only alive with anger and fear.

A malediction set upon him many years ago,

He now become infuriated from "love"

He gains always against it regret and sorrow.

He is lone now,

But he doesn't know is it possible but how?

He knows that his life now becomes dim

Wants someone who is always with him

His body is now dead from outside, becomes pale

But his heart still solace that everything is gonna be fine one day.

How much he would confort him.

All goes into vain.

He waits every day to sun be faded

He still waits for someone special to be reached.

"True Love is not something to express but It's from heart maybe in a distance but never apart."

12. I Don't Deserve You

I don't deserve you

I don't know How to say but yes It's true that I don't deserve you

you did everything to make me glee-

But What I did for you

"Nothing"

Except putting your life into threat

you deserve better for yourself

Even if I wanna recompense your all,I can never do this in my dreams.

what's the use of saying this now, it's absurd.

I don't be a burden on you anymore.

I want you to be happy in your life

because I don't deserve you at all.

you make my life brighter than star and beautiful than rainbow

but what I did for you

only I have been spoiling your life as just like the rain without rainbow,

no shine, no glory

only life long sorrow.

people say about you, I don't like-

because I know the true reason behind is me not you.

Do you know how much I cry at night

Sometimes it seems that my ribs is gonna be fill with my weeps.

No matter how much I cry, It always be less in front of my deeds.

I didn't even think that whatever I did what it leads-

How much I chided you

you didn't say a word

you believed in me, still have

But what I did,

I didn't even trust you

you always supported me, always gave me what I want

but I've only broken your heart

that's why I don't deserve you

" try to forgive me"

13. Do Your Best!

Do your best in whatever you want

No one is here to stop you from making choices

Be determined and fight against voices

for a moment think and to resolve

keep your mind strike on the goal

Any shackles which Bound you just throw it

Relax your mind,

Be fortitude too

That's it-

Just keep the whole process going strong as much as it can,

Definitely, nothing gonna happen wrong just try your best.

14. A TRUTH ABOUT YOU!

Can you guess this-
you are not worthless,
you have the ability to avoid anything
you're full of chaos, but you're still here to take it off from
yours
you're distinct from others
you don't need anyone qualities
coz you belong to yourself and that matters the most.

15. Imagine

I say a thing to you
That I don't know what to do
Every time just read a lot
Sitting standing writing such more
Except drawing and except sketching
I will be bright like UY scuti,
And yeah it's very spooky
Thanks and wish you happy
This is my imagination that I say to you just must change you!